THE
LIGHT BULB
and How It
Changed the World

THE
LIGHT BULB
and How It
Changed the World

Michael Pollard

Facts On File®

AN INFOBASE HOLDINGS COMPANY

Facts On File, Inc.
460 Park Avenue South
New York NY 10016

First published in the United States by Facts On File, Inc.
First published in the United Kingdom by Simon & Schuster Young Books.

Library of Congress Cataloging-in-Publication Data
Pollard, Michael, 1931–
    The light bulb and how it changed the world/Michael Pollard.
        p.   cm.   — (History and invention)
    Includes bibliographical references and index.
    ISBN 0–8160–3145–2
    1. Light bulbs—Juvenile literature.   2. Light bulbs—Social
aspects—Juvenile literature.   [1. Electricity.   2. Inventions.]
I. Title.   II. Series.
TK4351.P65   1995
621.3'09—dc20   94-15226

A CIP catalogue record for this book is available from the British Library

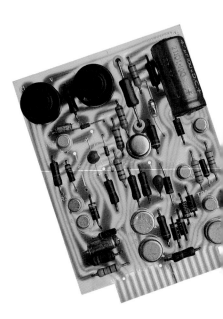

Picture Acknowledgements:
The publishers would like to thank the following for their permission to use copyright
material:
Advertising Archives: pp 19, 21, 28-29, 31, 34; Alcan: p 24b (Gillespie); Nick Birch: p 20;
British Telecom: p 18; Brown Brothers, USA: p 30t; Comstock: pp 40r, 41; Michael
Holford: pp 6cl, 12b; Hulton Deutsch Collection: pp 5, 13, 14, 17 (both), 27 (both), 30b,
32 (both); Image Bank: p 23; Peter Newark, Western Americana: p 15; Plastic Archive,
London: p 6cl; Popperfoto: pp 9t, 39, 40l; Rex Features; pp 6t, 8t, 24t 33 (both), 43b;
Science Photo Library; pp 6b, 7, 10, 11b, 12t, 16, 25, 36, 37tr and br, 42; Zefa: pp 8b, 9b,
22, 35, 38, 43t.

CONTENTS

Today's industrialized world depends on electricity as its main source of heat, light and power. We need light, so we press a switch. Electric machines carry out many of our domestic and personal tasks. Home entertainment and communications systems would not be available without electricity. Meanwhile, outside the home, foods are processed and goods are manufactured by electrical machinery. People in offices use an array of electrical devices to carry out their work. Modern railways run electric trains. Even tasks such as milking cows and grinding corn are performed with the help of electricity.

The pre-electric world

It is hard to believe that only about 120 years ago the world had no supply of electricity available. In 1880 the most effective form of lighting was by gas, either burning a naked flame or lighting up a "mantle" made of incandescent fabric. Gas was available only in towns and cities. In the country, people lit their homes with oil lamps or candles. They cooked on "ranges" that burned coal or wood and washed clothes in a boiler over a solid fuel fire. Open fires were the source of heat, but it was rare to heat rooms other than the kitchen and living-room.

Steam

The vast amounts of energy required by industry and the railways were provided by steam. It was made by boiling water over a solid fuel furnace and was used to move pistons inside cylinders and so drive a shaft. In factories, belts connected to the shaft transmitted energy to the machinery. In the steam locomotive, the only source of motive power on the railways, the shaft was connected to the driving wheels. The age of steam made the wheels of industry and transport turn for about 100 years.

This is one of Britain's most famous steam-powered trains, the *Flying Scotsman*, which ran daily between London and Edinburgh.

Ratcliffe-on-Soar power station in the English Midlands, part of the system that provides Britain with its electricity supply through a network of overhead cables.

Solid fuel

Before steam, heat and light energy were produced directly by burning solid fuel. Wood, coal, peat, charcoal, and mineral and vegetable oils were all burned. Town gas was made by burning coal and collecting the gases given off. Its invention made it possible to transport a source of energy through pipes to homes and factories, some distance from the gasworks where it was made. But gas has limited uses. A supply of energy with many uses had to wait for scientists to develop a way of providing a steady source of electricity. Even then they had to find a method of transmitting it along cables from the power station to the consumer.

The day that changed everything

From about the middle of the 19th century, scientists and inventors began to harness the power of electricity. The date of October 21, 1879 stands out. After many failed attempts, this was the day that the American inventor Thomas Alva Edison succeeded in making a length of chemically treated cotton, sealed inside a glass vacuum, glow continuously when an electric current was passed through it.

Edison had invented the electric light bulb. It gave a steadier and brighter light than anything previously known. It heralded a great revolution—the development of a supply system to bring electricity into every building in the industrialized world.

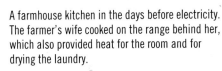

A farmhouse kitchen in the days before electricity. The farmer's wife cooked on the range behind her, which also provided heat for the room and for drying the laundry.

The New York skyline at night, dominated by the twin towers of the World Trade Center. In 1882 a street in New York City district was the first in the world to be lighted by electricity.

THE STRUGGLE TO UNDERSTAND

Electricity is a force which is part of the natural world. People have known about some of the effects of electricity for most of history, but until about 200 years ago the causes were a mystery. Lightning was a cause of wonder and fear in ancient civilizations, since it occasionally killed animals and people, destroyed trees and damaged buildings. Ancient peoples did not know that lightning is caused by electricity or that thunder is the sound made when the electricity is discharged. The Norse people of northern Europe believed that lightning and thunder were signs of the anger of the gods. Many people today are still superstitious about lightning.

Static electricity

Another electrical effect known to ancient peoples was the ability of certain materials, when rubbed, to attract others by static electricity. One of these materials is amber, a fossilized resin sometimes found on the seashore. The ancient Greek scientist Thales of Miletus wrote in about 600 BC about rubbing amber so that it would attract light objects such as pieces of straw or feathers. You can try this for yourself. If you rub the side of a plastic pen on your sweater, the pen will become energized with static electricity and will pick up small pieces of paper. The same effect explains how balloons stick to surfaces when rubbed against clothing.

Thales did not know the reason for this attraction, but merely reported it as a scientific curiosity. In doing so he used a word which the world was to find useful much later on. The ancient Greek word for amber is *elektron*, which gives us the words electricity and electron.

Amber is the resin from certain types of pine and other trees. It oozes from damaged trees and hardens in the open air. This piece of amber, with fossilized insects trapped inside, is about 40 million years old.

Science takes a hand

From about 1700 scientists began to take a greater interest in electricity. One idea was that an electric current could be produced by a "frictional machine." This was a device which generated a large static charge by rubbing a piece of material against a revolving glass globe.

A Dutch experimenter named Pieter van Musschenbroek discovered in 1746 that an electric shock was produced by passing an electrical charge through water. Meanwhile, in the United States, Benjamin Franklin carried out a famous but dangerous experiment in 1752 when he flew a kite in a thunderstorm with a key attached to the bottom of the string. When the kite was in the storm Franklin was able to obtain electric sparks from the key. This proved that lightning was an electrical force.

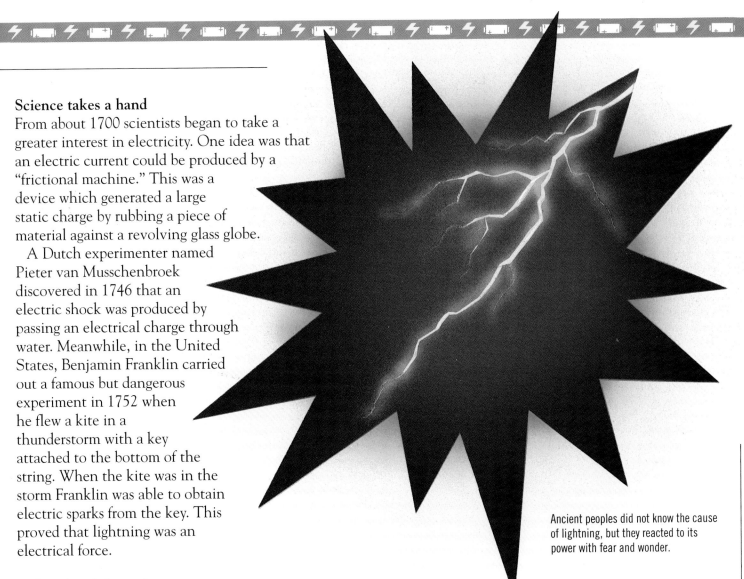

Ancient peoples did not know the cause of lightning, but they reacted to its power with fear and wonder.

Volta's breakthrough

All these experiments were of interest to scientists, but they did not result in a steady source of electricity. Nor had the experimenters any idea how such a source could be used if it were found. But in 1800 there was a breakthrough. An Italian scientist named Alessandro Volta discovered that a current could be produced by piling up alternate discs of copper and zinc interwoven with paper. Unlike the charge produced by the earlier experimenters, this current was continuous. Volta had invented the electric battery. As yet, however, there was no way of using the current it produced.

Alessandro Volta developed his discovery of chemical electricity into this "crown of cups," linked by wire. The cups contain heavily salted water. The metal plates, or electrodes, labeled Z are zinc, and those labelled S silver.

Until the early years of the 19th century, the study of electricity seemed to be leading nowhere. Alessandro Volta's battery was an interesting toy, but what could be done with it? No one as yet had any idea of how to use electricity. Experiments in laboratories seemed to offer nothing compared with the amazing achievements of the steam-engine, which were then just beginning. No one would have dreamed that within 100 years electricity would have brought about a revolution in communications, in home life, in industry and in transportation.

Use of the compass spread to Europe around AD 1200, and workshops making compasses sprang up around the major ports. This early example, with the compass rose floating in a wooden bowl, was made in the French port of Marseilles.

Hans Christian Oersted (1777–1851) was a professor of physics at Copenhagen University in Denmark when he made his important discovery.

Electricity and magnetism

In 1820 a Danish scientist made a discovery that was vitally important for the future of electricity. Hans Christian Oersted found that an electric current passing close to the magnetized needle of a compass made the needle move.

This discovery marked the true beginning of the electrical age. It meant that electrical energy could be converted into kinetic energy.

People had known since ancient times about magnetism and its use in the compass to aid navigation. Probably the first sailors to use a splinter of lodestone as a compass needle were Chinese, more than 4000 years ago. By about AD 1200, compasses were in general use by sailors all over the world.

Oersted had found the vital link between the ancient knowledge of magnetism and the newer discoveries about electricity.

Growth of the telephone

The adoption of the telephone in the United States was held back for many years by the huge distances which had to be covered by the network of telephone lines. It was not until 1915 that callers could speak directly from the Atlantic coast cities to those of the Pacific. In Europe, the Scandinavian countries led the way in the development of telephone services. By 1896 almost every village in Norway was connected by telephone. By 1914, a higher proportion of people in Denmark were connected by telephone than in any other European country.

Like the telegraph, the telephone opened up new employment opportunities for women. In the early days, when telephone equipment was primitive, it relayed the higher frequencies of women's voices more clearly than those of men. So women became the operators in telephone exchanges—dealing over the phone with callers—and women were also employed in business offices to make and receive calls. Other new jobs included making and maintaining the equipment and erecting the thousands of miles of lines required to carry calls. This gave employment to many men. By the 1920s the American Telephone and Telegraph Company alone had over 350,000 employees.

Training the work force

Since telecommunications was a new industry, it had to train its own work force, who often had only a very basic school education. This gave an impetus to technical education in such subjects as electrical engineering. The need for such highly-skilled people led eventually to the widening of the school curriculum to include science and, in some countries such as Germany, to the establishment of special technical schools.

In the early years of telephone service, operators had to connect each calling and receiving line with plugs and sockets. The caller asked the operator for the number required.

The network of telephone wires on New York's Broadway in 1887, before city lines were routed underground.

MAKING MONEY FROM TELECOMMUNICATIONS

The telecommunications industry was similar in one way to the railways. Before telegraph and telephone companies could earn any money from the services they provided, they had to spend huge sums on equipment, buildings and the networks of lines which linked their offices and exchanges. Services between continents depended on cables laid on the seabed at enormous expense, and all too often—as with the first telegraph cable across the English Channel and again with the first three cables across the Atlantic—the cables broke and all the investment was lost.

Ownership

In many countries governments took over the telephone and telegraph services. But in others such as the United States it was left to public companies to provide services. These companies had to raise large sums from shareholders to finance the building of their networks, and could prosper only if they had no competition.

The leading American telegraph company was Western Union, founded in 1851. It gained control of almost all telegraph business in the United States and then extended its activities abroad. Western Union failed to beat Alexander Graham Bell to the invention of the telephone. Bell's company, later called the American Telephone and Telegraph Company, was set up first. These two companies were later joined by another, the International Telephone and Telegraph Corporation.

For many years, these three giants controlled almost all telecommunications in the United States and had substantial interests overseas. Their shareholders did well, but the companies also plowed some of their massive profits back into other new businesses. In the 1920s AT&T, for example, developed today's leading sound system for motion pictures, Western Electric.

The network of lines in city streets eventually became so unsightly—and so vulnerable to damage in bad weather—that they were placed underground alongside other services such as gas and electricity.

Growth of telephone development in the United States

Dialing direct

A telephone system is far more complex than the telegraph. A telegraph service needed only one office in each town or village, with one line connecting it to the outside world. With the telephone, a separate line was needed for each customer, with a central exchange where connections could be made.

In the early days of the telephone, to make a call you had to ring the operator at the exchange, who would connect your line with the line of the person you wanted to speak to. A long-distance call involved relays from exchange to exchange and it often took several minutes to get through.

The dial telephone, invented by an American undertaker called Almon B. Strowger, put an end to this problem. He was worried that the operators in his home town were connecting customers to a rival business. He devised the dial telephone so that they could ring him direct. His "step by step" system of switches and relays remained in use throughout the world until the 1960s when electronic push-button, or touch-tone systems began to replace it.

Encouraging the public

The telegraph and telephone companies needed their systems to be used as much as possible. They devised many different ways of encouraging people to use them. For example, people could pay for and send birthday or wedding congratulations by telegram that arrived on a form like a greetings card. Faced with the problem of under-used lines during evenings and weekends when businesses were not operating, telephone companies introduced cheap rates for calls made at these times.

An American advertisement from the 1950s urging its readers to use the telephone

At 1:30 a.m. on October 21, 1879, a tense group of workers gathered in the laboratory of the inventor Thomas Alva Edison at Menlo Park, New Jersey. Edison was about to throw a switch which would send an electric current flowing through his latest invention—a glass vacuum globe containing a thin filament of carbon made by burning a thread of cotton. If Edison was right, he and his workers would witness the illumination of the first electric light bulb.

Brighter and brighter

Edison touched the switch and gradually the filament inside the glass began to glow, brighter and brighter. Tension in the laboratory gave way to excitement and admiration. The bulb went on glowing for 13 hours before the glass cracked. This was a minor problem. The glass could be made thinner and more resistant to heat. The important fact was that Edison had demonstrated a method of lighting that could eventually be installed in every home, every building, and every city street.

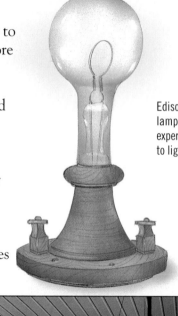

Edison's first electric lamp, a triumph of experiment which was to light up the world.

Light for everyone

Edison was well aware of the importance of his invention. He knew how difficult it was to read or do any kind of intricate work by the light of candles and oil lamps. The electric light bulb would revolutionize home life. But it was not enough to sell bulbs to every home. The electricity would have to be supplied as well. In 1879 there was no network of cables over or under streets carrying electricity and there was no central generating plant to supply it. Edison turned from inventing the light bulb to organizing a public electricity supply from generators which he designed himself.

The cost of building generators and wiring streets and individual buildings with insulated copper wire was enormous. Edison had to seek financial backing from the rich and powerful Morgan banking family, who virtually controlled the American railway system. Together they formed the Edison Electric Light Company to develop Edison's ideas.

Thomas Alva Edison's (1847–1931) laboratory where the first electric light bulb was created. The greatest challenge was to find the right material for the filament, a matter of chemical trial and error.

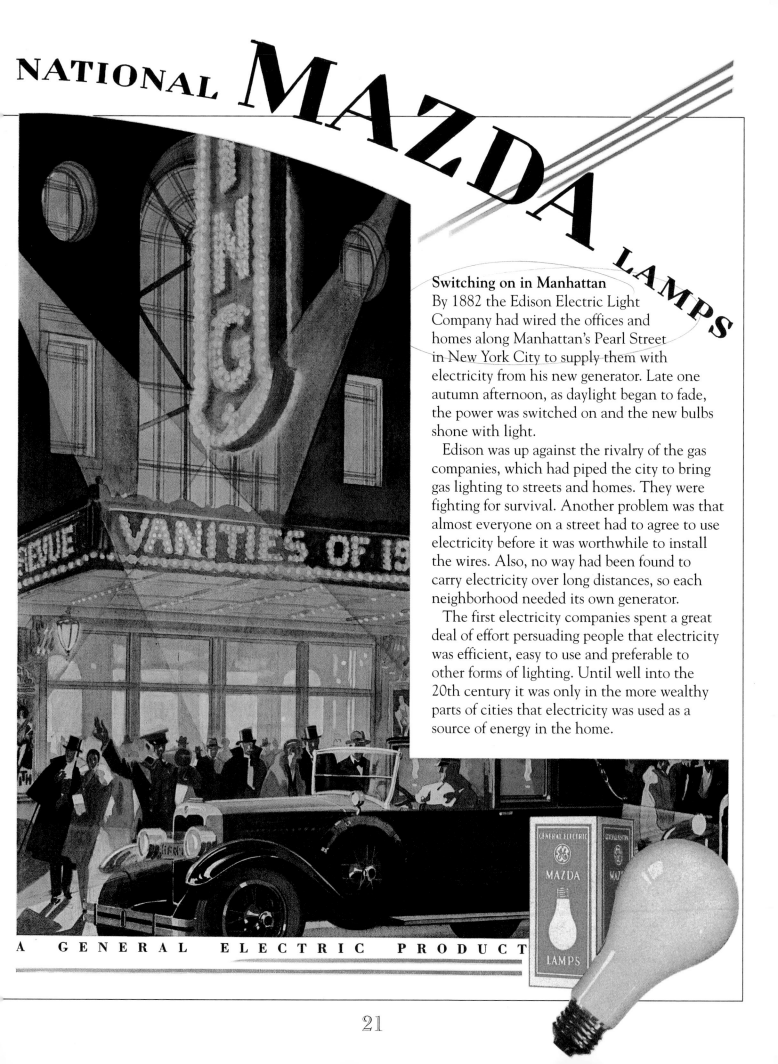

NATIONAL MAZDA LAMPS

Switching on in Manhattan

By 1882 the Edison Electric Light Company had wired the offices and homes along Manhattan's Pearl Street in New York City to supply them with electricity from his new generator. Late one autumn afternoon, as daylight began to fade, the power was switched on and the new bulbs shone with light.

Edison was up against the rivalry of the gas companies, which had piped the city to bring gas lighting to streets and homes. They were fighting for survival. Another problem was that almost everyone on a street had to agree to use electricity before it was worthwhile to install the wires. Also, no way had been found to carry electricity over long distances, so each neighborhood needed its own generator.

The first electricity companies spent a great deal of effort persuading people that electricity was efficient, easy to use and preferable to other forms of lighting. Until well into the 20th century it was only in the more wealthy parts of cities that electricity was used as a source of energy in the home.

A GENERAL ELECTRIC PRODUCT

SUPPLYING ELECTRICITY

Electricity is generated by changing kinetic energy into electrical energy. The moving parts of a generator must be driven by an energy source. The 19th-century producers of electricity like Edison turned to the source they knew best— steam raised by burning coal under a boiler. Steam pressure drove turbines which turned the moving parts of the generator. A high proportion of the world's electricity is still produced in this way, although steam is produced in many power stations by burning oil, natural gas or nuclear fuel.

Long-distance current

In the early days of electricity generation, a current had to be generated close to where it was used. The first power stations were small plants serving individual towns and cities. If there were coalfields nearby, electricity was inexpensive. If the expense of transporting coal over a distance had to be added, the electricity was costly.

The problem of transmitting electricity over distances was that a large amount of energy was lost as it traveled along the cables. If the current was transmitted at a high voltage, the loss of energy was far smaller. But a low voltage supply was necessary for safe use at home.

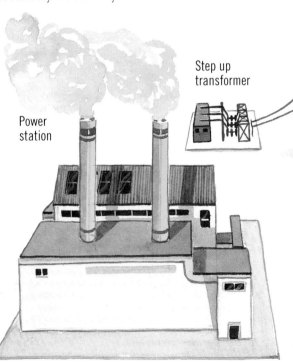

Power station

Step up transformer

Overhead pylons carry electricity

The development of systems of power transmission which could carry current over long distances enabled the production of electricity to be concentrated in fewer, larger power stations. To avoid energy loss, the current is increased to a high voltage for transmission and then decreased before it reaches the consumer.

The answer was the transformer, developed in both the United States and Hungary in the 1880s. This consisted of two coils of wire wound round an iron core. According to the number of turns in each coil, the voltage could be increased or decreased between them. The transformer enabled current to be transmitted long distances at a high voltage and then stepped down to a lower voltage for the consumer. Its development meant that power stations near sources of energy could supply electricity to places hundreds of miles away.

Water power

Once electrical engineers had overcome the problem of transmission it was possible to use another source of energy. Water had been used for thousands of years to drive grain mills. Hydroelectricity—electricity produced by falling water—brought together one of the world's oldest technologies with one of the newest. The heavy rainfall in mountainous areas is collected in reservoirs behind dams and then falls through pipes to the water turbines. Although water power itself is free, the investment in dams to provide a continuous supply of water to the turbines and the need to transmit the current to industrial and urban centers make the development of hydroelectricity costly.

The first demonstration of hydroelectricity was made in France in 1885. Electricity generated in Creil in northern France was transmitted to Paris, 32 miles away. By 1891 hydroelectricity was being carried 111 miles from Lauffen to Frankfurt in Germany. France, Italy, Switzerland and Canada were the leading countries in the introduction of hydroelectricity.

Power for development

Hydroelectric power is important for the industrial development of countries without resources of fossil fuels. The giant Aswan and Kariba dam projects in Africa have brought reliable power supplies to millions of people and stimulated industrial growth.

Over 75 percent of Canada's electricity is produced by water, and it costs only about half as much as electricity in Europe. Hydroelectricity also has the advantage that its production causes no pollution, although land has to be submerged to make way for the large reservoirs behind the dams.

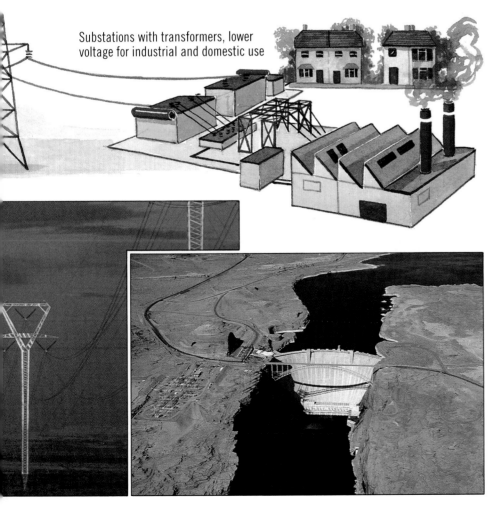

Substations with transformers, lower voltage for industrial and domestic use

Far left: Power lines in the United States. *Left:* The Glen Carron Dam in Arizona, which creates a water store for a huge hydroelectric power station.

The newly formed electricity companies of the 1880s and 1890s were anxious to persuade as many people as possible to use electric power. The more electricity was used, the quicker the companies would get back their huge investments in power stations and cables. Greater consumption would also bring down the price of electricity and, in turn, make it more attractive to new customers. Industry was the companies' main target.

Welding, only possible with the immense heat that could be generated by electricity, introduced industry to a new and more reliable way of joining metal to metal.

The pace of change

Enormous amounts of energy were used in mines, mills and factories. But industries such as iron and steelmaking and textile manufacture had invested heavily in steam power earlier in the century. They had originated in areas near coal supplies where the fuel for their steam boilers was cheap. They were not willing to make a change as long as their old equipment was working satisfactorily. One example of this was in the steel industry. An electric arc furnace, which made better quality steel, was invented as early as 1878, but it was another 40 years before it was widely used.

Going electric

Newer industries took to electricity more enthusiastically. The aluminum industry, for example, began in 1886 when an American chemistry student named Charles M. Hall discovered how to extract the metal from the clay-like rock bauxite. This process required high temperatures and relied on electricity. In 1894 the British Aluminum Company opened its own hydroelectric power station, in Foyers, Scotland to supply the aluminum plant next door. Within a few years the Foyers plant was making one-sixth of the world's aluminum.

The auto industry also used electricity from its beginning to power its welding equipment and machine tools. In the 1890s each car was hand-built in a small workshop, with each of its parts made separately. Cars were made only if an order had been placed by a customer. In 1906 in the United States, Henry Ford began building cars using mass-production methods.

The electric cells in which aluminum is extracted from its ore bauxite.

He believed correctly that there was a vast market for cars if the customers could pay their money and drive them away. When Ford opened his new car-making plant in Highland Park, near Detroit, as many of the production processes as possible were electrically powered. The speed and precision needed to turn out a line of identical vehicles with standardized parts could be provided only by electrically driven machines. In turn, the availability of electricity led to the development of new machine tools for the engineering industries.

Industry in the countryside
New industries were not tied to the coal-mining areas. They could manufacture products and package them anywhere if there was a supply of electricity. The result was the growth of what was called "light" industry in areas which had been dominated by farming. Industry paid better wages than farming. People in these areas were able to improve their standard of living by moving from farms to factories. New towns sprang up to house the new industrial workers.

In recent times many countries in Southeast Asia such as Taiwan and Malaysia have been able, with the help of electricity, to set up thriving industries and so free themselves from the poverty of economies based entirely on farming.

The auto industry was one of the first to use electricity in a big way, and has kept in the forefront of electric and electronic technology. On this Chrysler production line, computer-guided robots are spot-welding car bodies.

THE INDUSTRIAL POWER STRUGGLE

The development of electricity changed the course of history. The Industrial Revolution of the early 19th century, which replaced hand crafts with factory processes, had been powered by steam. Britain was also the birthplace of many major inventions of the Industrial Revolution, including the steam-engine itself. Untroubled by major wars for most of the 19th century, blessed with large reserves of coal and a large empire which provided markets for its goods, Britain became the world's leading industrial nation. It was often described as "the workshop of the world."

Industrial strength of the powers 1910

Cotton (kg per head)

Coal (tonnes per head)

Pig iron (kg per head)

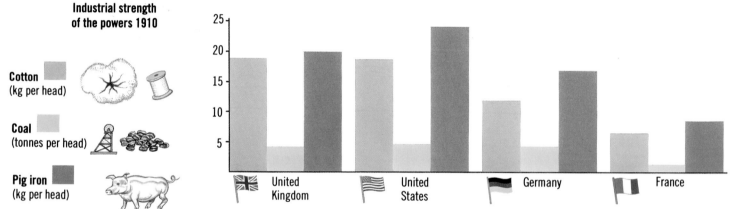

United Kingdom · United States · Germany · France

The league table

Britain's leadership began to slip away after 1880. With the end of the American Civil War in 1865, the United States began to develop its industrial power. Germany gained strength when its individual small states were united as one nation in 1870. But the most significant difference between the United States, Germany and Britain was in their readiness to use electricity once it became available. In the United States the use of electricity rose from 4 percent of all energy in 1899 to 40 percent by 1914. Meanwhile, British industries continued to use the older steam technology. An early attempt in 1887 to build a giant power station in London to bring electricity to the capital failed for lack of interest. Britain's rivals were eager to exploit the new opportunities provided by electricity.

It was mainly engineers from outside Britain who developed the means of bringing electricity into everyday use. Thomas Alva Edison created the world's first public electricity service. George Westinghouse, another American, was a pioneer in the building of electric power plants. In Germany, Ernst Werner von Siemens built the first electric railway.

The result was that by 1900 both the United States and Germany had overtaken Britain in the value of their industrial production, especially in

Finishing gun barrels at the giant Krupp armaments works in Essen, Germany in the early weeks of World War I. Germany was quick to adopt electric power for industrial processes, creating an industrial rivalry which was one of the causes of the war.

electrical manufacturing. By 1913 the United States was producing $296 million worth of electrical goods, and Germany was not far behind with $260 million. Britain, by comparison, produced only $120 million worth. In 1912, Britain used only one-seventh of the amount of electricity used in the United States.

In the marketplace

The United States and Germany showed great skill in developing world markets for their electrical industries. Singer sewing machines, Hoover vacuum cleaners, Remington typewriters and Kellogg's cornflakes were among the products that spread all over the world from American factories, and soon their companies set up overseas factories in Britain and elsewhere. German products that achieved similar worldwide fame included Frister and Rossman sewing machines, Yost typewriters and Krupp armaments.

Envy and war

Industrial rivalry between the major world powers, spurred on by the development of electricity, was one of the causes of World War I. Mass production of goods in electrically powered factories demanded new markets. Britain had a ready-made market in its empire, but it was no longer producing goods that the markets wanted to buy. Struggling to build its own empire, Germany looked at Britain with envy, which gradually turned to aggression. Britain resented Germany's growing industrial might. In August 1914, rivalry turned to war.

Model T Fords fresh off the production line at Ford's American factory in 1925. Electric power for machine tools was vital to the Ford system of mass production.

Electricity was first supplied to homes to provide them with a better form of lighting. At first, only the wealthy homeowners could afford it. The cost of wiring a house for electricity was too great for poorer families, and their landlords were not prepared to pay for it. So electricity in the home made a slow start. Most people had to put up with older methods of lighting—gas in the towns, and candles or oil lamps in the country.

Electricity does the work

New houses began to be built with electric wiring already in place during the 1920s. By this time, manufacturers were coming up with a range of electric appliances for the home, encouraged by the electricity supply industry, which wanted to sell more current.

Sweeping rooms with brushes was hard work, and often created as much dust as it cleared away. The electric vacuum cleaner sucked the dust into a bag, which could then be emptied—disposable bags came later. It made housework easier and less frustrating.

The electric cleaner was invented in 1905, but it was not until the 1930s that it was seen in most homes.

The electric iron was an even more popular appliance. Previously, heavy irons had to be heated over a solid fuel range or gas stove. The electric iron was lighter and provided continuous heat.

The electric toaster was another early innovation. An ever-increasing flow of appliances followed.

The manufacture of electrical appliances for the home was a completely new industry that began in the early 1900s, but grew rapidly in the 1920s and 1930s.

Advertising was used heavily to sell the benefits of these appliances to the consumer. Electricity companies were eager to cooperate since the more appliances that were sold, the more electricity was used.

More freedom for women

Makers of electrical goods claimed that they were clean and saved effort. This was certainly true. A room could be cleaned using a vacuum cleaner in a fraction of the time and much more effectively than with a brush and dustpan. There was no danger of clothes ironed electrically picking up smuts from the iron.

Electric cooking and fires did away with the need to carry coal around the house and clear ashes. Small appliances saved endless effort in preparing food, and refrigerators prevented food from going to waste.

Home life improved, especially for women on whom the main burden of domestic work fell. Looking after the house was no longer a full-time job. Many women were freed to go out to work, or to take part in social activities in the daytime. Organizations sprang up to provide interesting activities for women. Women took up an interest in politics, found time to read books from the library, or helped with voluntary charity work. The beginning of today's increasing role for women in social and political life can be traced to their liberation from time-consuming domestic chores by electricity.

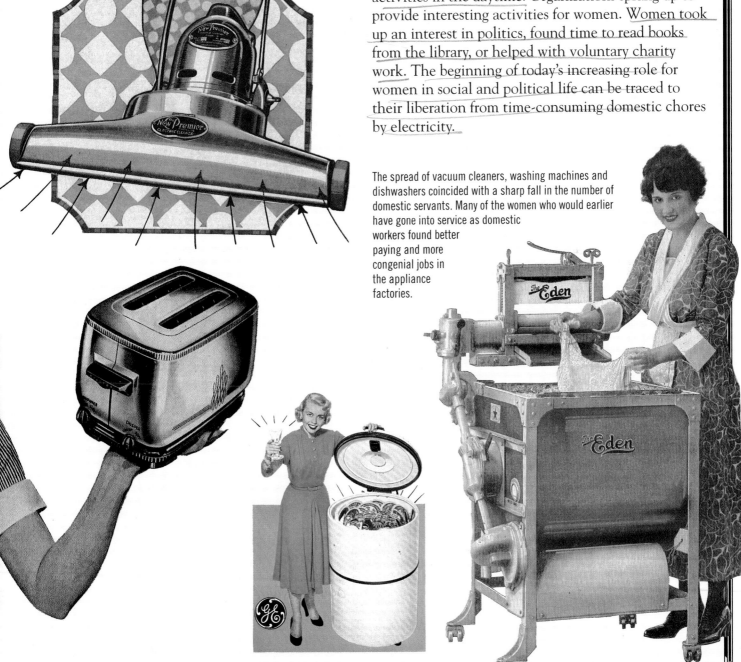

The spread of vacuum cleaners, washing machines and dishwashers coincided with a sharp fall in the number of domestic servants. Many of the women who would earlier have gone into service as domestic workers found better paying and more congenial jobs in the appliance factories.

In 1864 a Scottish scientist, James Clerk Maxwell, suggested that waves of electricity traveled through space like the waves of light. Maxwell's idea sparked off a wave of experiment and invention that gave the world radio and television. By 1887 a German scientist, Heinrich Hertz, had proved that waves of electricity called radio waves are indeed part of the electromagnetic spectrum that includes light waves.

The first radio

In 1895 a young Italian student, Guglielmo Marconi, began experimenting with radio waves in the garden of his home. He built the world's first radio set and sent messages over it in Morse code. He had invented radio-telegraphy.

Finding little interest in his invention at home in Italy, Marconi took it to Britain. By 1898 he had managed to send a radio message in Morse from France to England, and three years later he sent a similar message across the Atlantic.

The introduction of radio in the 1920s sparked off a wave of enthusiasm and wonder. To receive speech and music out of the air seemed like a miracle. *Inset*: Soon the wonder turned sour when dictators like Adolf Hitler began to use radio as a weapon of war.

Television seemed an even greater miracle, although we would not be satisfied today with the quality of the pictures. The screen was postcard-size, and the picture was disrupted by lines and frequent breakdowns.

The birth of television

By 1927 John Logie Baird, a Scottish engineer, had managed to reproduce a picture of a human face, transmitted by radio waves. He named it "television." His system was dropped in favor of a better one invented by a Russian scientist working in the United States called Vladimir Zworykin. By 1938 there were television services in the United States, Germany, Britain and Russia. The pictures were in black and white, and their quality was very poor by today's standards. But from then on there were regular improvements, such as better cameras, bigger pictures and color, which led to modern high-quality television pictures.

Words by radio

Countries could now communicate with each other by telegraph without having to lay cables under the sea. Ships could send radio messages to each other and to stations on shore. Marconi's system could not carry speech or music, but another invention called the radio valve was more sensitive to radio waves. As early as 1904 there was an experimental radio broadcast of music in Austria, but it was not until about 1920 that radio stations in Canada, the United States and Europe began to make regular broadcasts. By 1927 there were nearly 600 radio stations broadcasting speech and music in the United States, and about 200 in Europe.

Windows on the world

Radio and television provide entertainment in the home, but they also offer much more. People can see and hear news events as they take place. They can see Olympic athletes breaking records, hear minute-by-minute commentaries on football games, and share in the joys and horrors of what is happening in the world.

Television in particular has had an effect on world affairs. The horrors of the Vietnam War in the 1960s and 1970s, viewed nightly at home, convinced Americans that it must be brought to an end. Pictures of starvation in East Africa in the 1980s resulted in massive fund-raising efforts. The way politicians look on television can win or lose an election. Thanks to electricity, people know more about the world they live in.

In 1831 Michael Faraday discovered that motion could be produced by an electric current, and electric current by motion. Inventors began to apply this knowledge to transport. Their first efforts were battery-operated railways. These showed that electric traction was possible, but the batteries were too heavy, too big, and ran low too quickly for these projects to succeed. The breakthrough came in 1879.

The first electric railway

The German Siemens company demonstrated a train powered by an electric motor in 1879. The current was supplied from a generator through a third rail and the running rails provided the negative connection. Two years later, a short electric train service was opened in Lichterfelde, Germany. Other engineers took up the idea, and an American named Frank Sprague devised a way of supplying the current from overhead wires.

Road and rail

As in industry, the railways had invested heavily in steam power, and the change to electricity was slow. The railway companies made most of their profit from hauling freight, and electric locomotives were not yet powerful enough to cope with heavy long-distance haulage. Once powerful electric motors appeared most of the world's railways converted to electric traction for high-speed, long-distance lines as well as for local and suburban services.

Underground electric railways developed more quickly. Although there were no cars or trucks on the roads, many cities were choked with horse-drawn traffic. It made good sense to carry passengers underground. Electric locomotives could accelerate and slow down faster than steam-engines. They were ideal for inner-city travel with its frequent stops and starts.

City traffic jams are not merely a modern nuisance, as this photograph taken in Chicago in 1905 shows. It was to try to cure problems like this that underground railways were built.

A work gang lays rail lines along London's Embankment, beside the Thames River, in 1908. Railways seemed a good idea at the time, but as other road traffic increased, trains often caused obstruction—as in the Chicago scene above.

The first electric underground railway opened in London in 1890. It was followed by similar systems in Glasgow, Berlin, Paris, Budapest and Hamburg. The first electric underground railway in the United States, the New York Subway, opened in 1904.

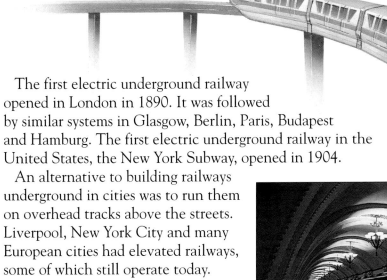

An alternative to building railways underground in cities was to run them on overhead tracks above the streets. Liverpool, New York City and many European cities had elevated railways, some of which still operate today.

Meanwhile, trains had made their appearance in many city streets— New York, Boston and Philadelphia. Horse-drawn systems were replaced by trains drawn by electric power, which became commonplace. Rail travel was quiet, pollution-free and cheap. A later development was the trolleybus, which also took its power from overhead lines but did not need rails.

Cars of the future?

In one important area of transport, electricity has so far not been successful. Many attempts have been made to develop an electric car operated by batteries, but technology has not yet been able to provide speed and long mileage. The only successful battery-operated road vehicles have been small delivery vans for door-to-door deliveries in towns and cities. These do not need to move quickly, and make journeys of only a few miles before their batteries can be recharged overnight.

The advantages of electric cars would be massive savings in oil resources, pollution by exhaust fumes would be eliminated, and the cars would be almost silent. Many of the world's leading car manufacturers are now working on plans to electrify road travel.

Moscow's underground railway system, opened in the 1930s, was the most efficient in the world in its early years. Its designers and engineers, mostly from Western Europe, had built in the experience gained from systems in Britain, France and Germany.

General Motors' *Sunraycer*, one of the many experimental cars designed to run on solar power. So far, no one has been able to crack the problem of collecting enough solar energy to power long journeys.

Alessandro Volta invented the first electric cell to produce a current through chemical action in 1800. For over 30 years batteries—single electric cells linked together—were the only way of producing a continuous electric current. Although many different types were made in the 19th century, they were rarely used outside of scientific laboratories. Everyday uses for electricity had not yet been developed, and the energy output from batteries was too small for practical purposes. Once electricity could be generated, it looked as if the battery might become obsolete.

Light where you need it

The invention of the light bulb changed all that. In 1888 the first "dry cell" appeared, which could be carried more easily because it contained chemical paste instead of a liquid. Two or more dry cells connected and packaged together to make a battery, with a miniature light bulb, made up the flashlight. People had a new and more convenient way of lighting their way at night, to replace oil or candle lanterns.

The use of dry cells has gradually widened until today they power a wide range of devices such as toys, electric shavers, radios, cassette players and small laptop computers. Collections of cells linked together to make power packs are used by explorers, oil prospectors and other travelers in remote areas to provide electricity for lighting and communications. Batteries also enable people who live in areas where there is no public electricity supply to keep in touch with the world. Modern dry cells give many hours of continuous power, and some can be recharged by connecting them to the main supply through a transformer.

Chemical electricity, supplied by batteries, provides a portable power supply. Now used to power a wide range of appliances, it first found popularity as the source of energy for flashlights, replacing paraffin lanterns.

WARNING!
Never try to recharge a battery from the main supply unless you have a charger designed for the purpose and you have checked that the batteries are of the rechargeable type. Other types of battery may catch fire or explode.

Starting the car

Rechargeable batteries of the older "wet" type are used in cars, vans and trucks. They provide power for the engine's starter motor and supply current to the lights and other devices when the engine is switched off. Car batteries are kept charged by a small generator operated by the engine when it is running.

Wet batteries are also carried on ships, aircraft and some trains to provide power when their engines are not running. Many buildings such as offices and hotels, cinemas and airports have an emergency supply of battery electricity for use if the main supply breaks down. Spacecraft and space satellites carry batteries that provide power for communications and other functions. These are recharged by solar power.

Although batteries supply only a tiny proportion of the electricity used in the world, they are a source of portable electricity and greatly add to the convenience of modern life. For people in remote, rural areas they are a lifeline.

Power on your wrist

The story of electric batteries has been one of miniaturization. Many small devices such as wrist watches, which need only a small current to keep them going, are powered by tiny button batteries. These can last up to a year or even longer.

Batteries enable us to use electrical devices when we are on the move or away from a main supply. Most batteries are disposable once their energy is exhausted, but for environmental reasons rechargeable batteries are becoming more popular.

The history of electricity since the 1960s has been dominated by the development of space and computer technologies. The launch of the first space satellite, *Sputnik I*, in 1957 set off a space race between the United States and the former Soviet Union. Spacecraft needed sophisticated navigation and guidance systems, both on board and at their control stations on earth for communications. The calculations involved in space navigation could not be made fast enough by the human brain. The result was a leap forward in the development of computers. Room for equipment on board was limited, so miniaturized equipment was needed, to be operated by batteries charged by solar energy.

Electronics

Everyone has benefited from the scientific strides forward that were made during the space race. The transistor, much less prone to failure than the radio valve, is now a standard component in radios, televisions, cassette and compact disc players. The silicon chip contains hundreds of electronic components on a piece of material only a few thousands of an inch across. It is a vital component of computers, video recorders and even washing machines. Apart from their convenient small size, transistors and silicon chips operate efficiently on much lower power than previous devices. The battery-powered Walkman, for example, would not be possible without transistors and silicon chips.

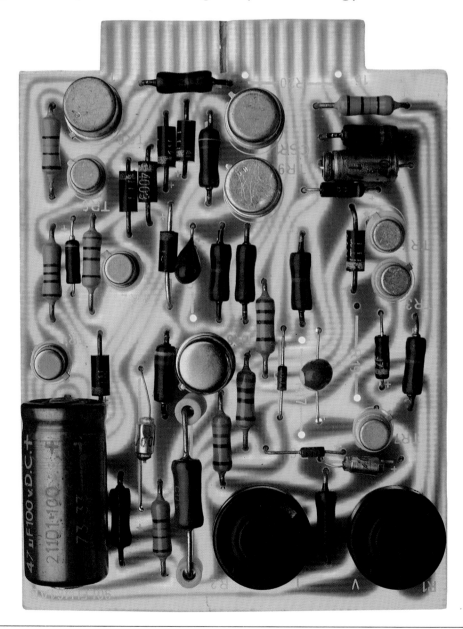

The invention of the transistor enabled very complex electrical circuits to be compressed into a small space. This is the transistor circuit of a battery-powered smoke detector which is about half the size of a postcard.

News from space

The space race has now slowed down. This is partly because it was a propaganda weapon in the Cold War between the United States and Soviet Union which ended with the breakup of the Soviet Union in 1989. Also, the huge cost of space exploration is a burden even to rich countries like the United States. But the space race improved communications to earth from the satellites that have been put into space.

Most people know satellites best as the source of television programs that are beamed up from earth and then relayed to satellite receiving dishes. But they have many other uses. Shipping and aircraft rely on them for help with navigation. By sending back television pictures of the earth and its atmosphere, satellites help with weather forecasting and predicting long-term climatic changes. Satellites also carry news pictures, telephone conversations and fax messages between distant points on the earth with far greater clarity than cable or earth radio communication.

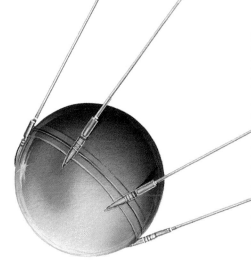

The world's first communications satellite, *Sputnik 1.* Its batteries lasted for only a few hours, but it marked the beginning of a new chapter in communications.

Seeing things happen

News from abroad on television has usually been sent by satellite. We often see it as it actually happens. This has altered the way people think about events taking place in other countries. For example, in 1989 the Soviet empire in Eastern Europe, controlled by the USSR in Moscow, began to break up into its older separate parts. Satellite pictures of the old leaders being overthrown inspired other Eastern European countries to join in the movement for independence. Similarly, satellite pictures of the brutal repression by the Chinese government of student protest in Beijing in the same year outraged people everywhere. But satellites carry good news too. Thanks to pictures relayed by them, we can all share the thrills of an Olympic crowd as records are broken, or enjoy a concert performed on the other side of the world.

The *Aurora II* communications satellite was launched in May 1991. It provides a satellite link for telephone and television networks between Alaska and the rest of the United States.

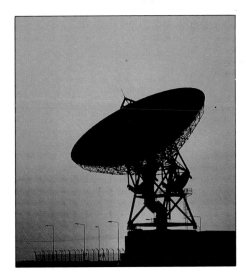

A satellite receiving dish in the Middle East. It collects signals bounced via satellite from transmitters in other parts of the world, and feeds them into local telecommunications networks.

For many years after electricity became the main source of power in the home, most people thought of it as a "clean" form of energy. It is clean to use, since electric motors do not give off exhaust fumes and electric fires do not create smoke. But electricity generated by power stations using coal, oil, natural gas or nuclear fuel is not clean to make.

Acid rain

Power stations burning non-nuclear fuel emit chemical gases. These rise high into the atmosphere and can travel hundreds of miles before releasing the chemicals elsewhere as "acid rain." The acid destroys trees and robs many wild creatures of their habitats. When acid rain falls into rivers and lakes it can poison the water.

Acid rain is an international problem because the chemicals emitted by power stations in one country affect the environment in another. Solving the problem depends on agreement between countries to clean the emissions from power stations before they are released into the atmosphere. This is not difficult to do, but it adds to the expense of generating electricity.

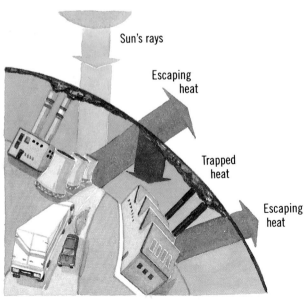

Sun's rays

Escaping heat

Trapped heat

Escaping heat

Chemical emissions from power stations and factories do not escape the earth's atmosphere. They are trapped by the sun's heat and travel around in the atmosphere, to be deposited on the surface again as acid rain.

It's winter in Poland, but these stunted trees will never carry buds when spring comes. They are dead—victims of acid rain caused by emissions from power stations in Western Europe.

The Chernobyl nuclear power station in the Ukraine under construction. In April 1986 there was an explosion at Chernobyl which released nuclear contamination into the atmosphere, spreading radioactivity throughout northwestern Europe.

Nuclear nightmare

Using nuclear fuel to generate electricity raises another set of problems. Nuclear power stations produce highly dangerous radioactive materials which must be controlled and contained. If the systems in the power station overheat, radioactivity can escape into the atmosphere and travel hundreds of miles in the air.

This is what happened at Chernobyl in the Ukraine in 1986. The nuclear fission process producing the heat for the boilers ran out of control. There was an explosion which badly damaged the power station and released radioactivity which spread across northern and north western Europe. The effects of radioactive contamination, which include leukaemia and birth defects, may not show up for many years.

Accidental radioactive leaks are not the only dangers from nuclear power stations. The water used in generating is discharged, usually into the sea. Many people believe that the water's warmth and traces of radioactivity may have an effect on the environment.

Nuclear waste

The fuel used in nuclear power stations is uranium. When it is "spent" it becomes waste material and has to be disposed of. It cannot be dumped like ash from a coal-fired station because the spent uranium is still radioactive and will remain so for many years. Scientists believe that it can safely be stored underground, but this raises two more questions. Can it be transported safely to the storage site? And who would be happy to have a store of nuclear waste near their home?

There is also the question of what will happen when a nuclear power station is too old to be efficient. Any other kind of building can be demolished and the land used for something else. A nuclear plant and the land it is built on will remain dangerously radioactive, perhaps for hundreds of years. The only answer seems to be to seal the old plant in a thick layer of concrete and leave it standing. The lives of people in 100 years' time may be affected by how we generate the electricity we use today.

Throughout most of the 19th century, the leading industrial countries in Europe and North America were those with good supplies of raw materials for manufacturing and coal to produce steam power. They were able to sell their products to other countries lacking these resources. Britain had a ready-made market in its empire, which covered almost one-quarter of the earth's surface. The United States had political and economic agreements with the countries of Central and South America where it bought raw materials and sold products. Germany had a small empire but wanted a bigger one, an ambition that led to two world wars.

Industrial newcomers

Things have changed since World War II ended. Older industrial countries like the United States and Britain, which had strained their economies to win the war, lost their ability to stay ahead. Just as electricity enabled industries to start up on new sites in the late 19th century, in the post-war years it gave some countries new freedom to join in the world industrial race.

Japan

Despite having to import all its fuel supplies and its defeat in World War II, Japan was the first country to take advantage of the new political situation. Japanese industry was strong before the war, but most of its effort was concentrated on armaments. A Japanese businessman named Konosuke Matsushita had begun making electrical goods and exporting them as far back as 1916. After 1945 he had to rebuild his business from scratch. He carefully researched what products people needed and how much they were prepared to pay. By the time he died in 1989 Matsushita electrical and electronic goods, under a variety of brand names, had swept the world. Other Japanese manufacturers had similar success by keeping their eyes closely on their markets. Japanese cars, for example, fiercely attacked the big car companies of Europe and North America, partly by fitting as standard equipment items which other manufacturers treated as optional extras. Japanese products have such a good reputation for value that some electronic products made in Europe are even sold with Japanese-sounding labels on them.

Konosuke Matsushita (1894–1989) started building up his electronics empire by copying Western products. After 1945 he saw that the way to keep ahead of Western industry was to offer better quality and greater choice.

A shopping mall in Singapore, Southeast Asia. Singapore once gained its prosperity as a trading port and naval base. Today it is the center of thriving industry, made possible by the availability of electricity.

The Pacific Basin

Other countries in the Far East and the Pacific Basin learned quick lessons from Japan. They could produce consumer goods far cheaper than Americans or Europeans, and their products were at least as good. They could even produce the goods and let Americans or Europeans sell them. This book is written on a computer which is sold by an American company, but parts of it were made in South Korea, Singapore, Japan and other Pacific Basin and Far Eastern countries. Electricity has freed the world's industry from domination by North America and Europe.

Africa next?

With its rivers and mountains, Africa has great prospects for the generation of hydroelectricity. Some projects such as the Tana River Development in Kenya have already started. Many parts of Africa are also rich in resources of raw materials for industry. It could be that in the next century a new industrial revolution will take place in Africa, just as the formerly mainly agricultural economies of the Far East have changed in the 20th century.

Aswan Dam

Nile

Congo

Lake Kariba

Zambezi

Africa is blessed with many large rivers. This map shows some which have been dammed to provide electricity.

ELECTRICITY FOR THE FUTURE

Most of the world's electricity comes from non-renewable materials. These include coal, oil and natural gas—the fossil fuels. Scientific estimates of when they will be used up vary, but oil and natural gas could begin to run out some time in the next century. Even nuclear power depends on a non-renewable source, uranium. Electricity can also be generated from renewable resources. The most widely used of these at present is falling water. Other renewable resources include wind, wave, tidal and solar power.

Blowing in the wind

Wind-power was used for hundreds of years to drive pumps for irrigation and mills for grinding corn. It can also drive an electric generator. Modern versions of windmills with light metal blades are built individually, to provide electricity for an isolated farm or small settlement, or in collections called "wind farms." Wind farms feed the electricity they generate into the public supply. The most ambitious wind farm project so far has been built in California.

A wind farm near Palm Springs, California. Although the amount of power that can be generated from wind turbines is small, the technology is still fairly new and engineers are working on making it more effective.

Right: The Rance tidal power plant in France. As the tide flows in and out of the river estuary, it produces kinetic energy in the barrier which is converted into electrical energy in the same way as in a hydroelectric power station.

Solar power

The sun is a vast and unending source of heat energy that can be harnessed to generate electricity. The space race of the 1950s and 1960s saw the sun's energy being used to recharge the batteries of spacecraft. One of the by-products of this research was the tiny solar cell used in many of today's watches and calculators.

Each solar cell produces only a small current, but cells can be linked together in panels. In parts of Africa and India, panels of solar cells provide enough electricity to power village television sets. Elsewhere, solar cells are used to power lighthouses and radio beacons.

Panels of solar cells can also be grouped together in large arrays. California has several solar power stations like this, each generating enough electricity to supply a small town.

Another way of using solar power is to concentrate the sun's rays in mirrors that focus them on a boiler. The boiler produces steam to drive a turbine. There are solar power stations of this type in California, Russia and France. Large installations like this are very expensive to build, but are easy to maintain and their energy source comes free.

Energy on the tide

On every ocean coastline in the world, the tide flows in and out twice each day. It is another free source of energy. Rance, near St. Malo in France, is the world's largest tidal power station. It harnesses the energy of the tide's rise and fall in the estuary of the Rance river. The water drives generators like the falling water in a hydroelectric plant.

Collecting solar energy to generate electricity at a solar power station in France. Mirrors reflect the sun's rays on to the collector tower, generating heat that operates a generator turbine.

Other countries are interested in tidal power, but there are great difficulties. A tidal barrier producing enough power to be worthwhile would need to be several miles long. It would be unsightly and could present a hazard to shipping. But the Rance plant shows that tidal power is a possibility for the future.

Looking ahead

Interest in renewable, alternative energy sources has increased since the 1970s, when it was realized that fossil fuel supplies would eventually run out. Renewable energy so far contributes only a tiny fraction to the world's electricity requirements. But the technology is now available to generate electricity from natural resources without the pollution and other problems caused by non-renewable resources.

Glossary

acid rain Rain containing chemicals which damage or destroy living things.

ambassador The representative of one country who lives in another and looks after his own country's interests.

bauxite A clay-like substance found in the ground from which the metal aluminum is extracted.

brand name A name, such as Hoover or Toyota, which manufacturers give to their own products.

button battery A miniature electric battery used to power small devices such as watches.

disposable bags Bags made of paper or plastic which are thrown away after use.

dry cell The single unit of an electric battery which uses a chemical paste as the electrolyte.

electric arc furnace A device for making steel by using the immense heat produced when a strong electric current is made to "jump" or arc across a small gap.

electric battery Two or more electric cells linked together.

electromagnet A coil of wire wound round an iron rod. The rod becomes magnetic when an electric current is passed through the wire.

electromagnetic spectrum The range of electromagnetic waves which stretches from very long waves such as those that carry long wave radio to very short waves such as X rays and microwaves.

elevated railway A railway built above street level.

exhaust The poisonous fumes given off by internal combustion engines.

fax An electronic device for sending visual messages along telephone lines.

fossil fuel Fuel such as coal, natural gas, oil or peat which comes from plant or animal matter that decayed millions of years ago.

generator A machine for making electricity by turning a shaft inside an arrangement of coils. The movement of the shaft produces electricity in the coils.

hydroelectricity Electricity produced by using the power of falling water to turn the shaft of a generator.

insulate To cover an electric wire with plastic, rubber or other material to prevent the escape of electricity.

kinetic energy Energy produced by movement.

leukemia A serious, often fatal, disease caused by too many white corpuscles in the blood.

mantle A device made of chemically treated cotton which glows when it is fitted to a lighted gas supply.

mass production A system of factory production in which machines are assembled from stocks of identical parts.

navigation The skill of finding the way using observation of the stars or sun or aids such as maps and compasses.

nuclear fission The process of splitting atoms to release energy.

peat A fossil fuel made of decayed plant matter.

pig iron An oblong mass of iron produced by smelting iron ore in a furnace.

piston The part of an engine in which the pressure of gases is made to move a cylinder which in turn is connected to a shaft.

radioactivity Energy given off when atoms decay or are split.

rechargeable battery A portable source of electricity which can be given new life by connecting it to household current through a charger.

reserves Unused stocks of fossil fuel.

silicon chip A thin wafer of silicon mineral which can be used to carry electrical circuits.

solar power Electric power obtained by using the energy given off by the sun to heat water and produce steam that drives a generator.

static electricity A force which attracts objects to each other by the transfer of electrons.

technical school A school where the students specialize in subjects such as engineering.

tidal power Electric power obtained by using the movement of the tides to drive a generator.

transformer A device which increases or decreases the strength of an electric current. It contains two separate coils of wire wound around an iron core.

transistor A small component of many electrical appliances, such as radio and television sets, which carries out a variety of functions such as amplifying sound.

transmit Send.

wind farm A collection of small generators which make electricity by using wind power to drive them.

zinc A bluish-white metal used in many electrical devices, and for plating iron to prevent it from rusting.

INDEX

FURTHER READING

Gardner, Robert. ELECTRICITY (New York: Simon and Schuster Trade, 1993).

Glover, David. BATTERIES, BULBS AND WIRES: Science Facts and Experiments (New York: Kingfisher, 1993).

Robson, Pam. ELECTRICITY (New York: Watts, Franklin, Inc., 1993).

Spangenburg, Ray and Kit Moser. THE HISTORY OF SCIENCE FROM 1895–1945 (New York: Facts On File, 1994).

————— . THE HISTORY OF SCIENCE FROM 1946 to the 1990s (New York: Facts On File, 1994).